STAND UP, STAND OUT!

THE ILLUSTRATORS

Anna Higgie

Anna is an Australian-born illustrator now living and working in Bristol, England. She spends most of her time in her Stokes Croft studio, where she uses a combination of traditional and digital techniques to create her illustrations.

Anna Stiles

London-born Anna first studied French in college before becoming an illustrator in 2009. Anna makes detail-rich, hand-drawn illustrations and is especially interested in detail and mark making. She mostly works in ink and paint.

Jessica Singh

Jessica is from Australia and is a graduate of Central Saint Martins in London, England. Inspired by her Indian heritage, she loves vibrant color and traditional textile designs. When she's not drawing, Jessica loves traveling, and walking.

Jonny Wan

Jonny was born in Sheffield but now lives and works in Manchester, England. Failure to grow beyond 5 ft. 7 in. saw his dreams of a multimillion dollar salary playing basketball dashed, so he decided to pursue the next best thing—illustration!

Kelly Thompson

After an initial career in fashion photography, Kelly began to capture her subjects as ephemeral illustrations. As a freelance artist, Kelly first works by hand, sketching up in pencil, before using Photoshop and adding color with help from her trusty Wacom.

Taylor Dolan

Taylor was born in America but recently graduated with an MA degree in children's book illustration which brought her to Cambridge, England. She is happiest working at her drawing table, with a good audiobook and some kind of chocolatey snack.

Sofia Bonati

Born in Argentina, Sofia now lives in the United Kingdom. She first studied geology before completing a degree in graphic design and illustration. To her soft pencil drawings she likes to add inks, watercolor, and gouache —making her portraits elegant and refined.

Margarida Esteves

Margarida is a Portuguese illustrator based in London, England. Her work is colorful, layered, textured, and detailed. She likes to mix traditional and digital techniques. When she is not working, you will find her watching movies and reading about history.

THIS IS A WELBECK CHILDREN'S BOOK

First published in 2020 by Welbeck Children's Limited
An imprint of the Welbeck Publishing Group
20 Mortimer Street, London W1T 3JW

Text, design and illustration © Welbeck Children's Limited 2020

All rights reserved. This book is sold subject to the condition that it may not be reproduced, stored in a retrieval system or transmitted in any form or by any means, electronic, mechanical, photocopying, recording or otherwise, without the publisher's prior consent.

ISBN: 978-1-78312-860-0
Printed in Dongguan, China

1 3 5 7 9 10 8 6 4 2

Historical Consultant: Lucinda Hawksley

Executive Editors: Alexandra Koken and Bryony Davies
Design Manager: Emily Clarke
Design: Ceri Hurst
Production: Jack Matts

STAND UP, STAND OUT!

25 REBEL HEROES
WHO STOOD UP FOR THEIR BELIEFS
— AND HOW THEY COULD INSPIRE YOU

KAY WOODWARD

WELBECK

CONTENTS

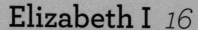
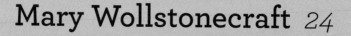

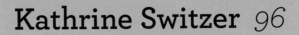 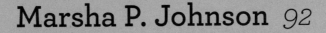

Introduction

Some people are happy to watch the world go by. And that's all right. The world's a pretty amazing place.

But some people aren't content just to be observers. If they see something that upsets them, they stand up and speak out about it. They *do* something. It doesn't matter if they're a president or a slave, a queen or a teenager, each one of them has the chance to make a difference. And guess what? You can read about 25 of them in this book!

Whiz back in time to find out all about **Spartacus**—a slave who wasn't very big on fighting to the death just to entertain the Roman crowds. Meet **Galileo Galilei**, who made astonishing discoveries about the universe in the 1600s. He was then told to shut up about them, but did he? Of course not.

Find out about some truly fabulous leaders, including **Elizabeth I**, the English queen, who proved skeptics wrong when she showed that a woman could rule a country just as well as a man, if not better. There's **Abraham Lincoln**, the American president who was determined to abolish slavery in the United States. And then there's **Nelson Mandela**, who fought against apartheid (segregation) in South Africa and became the country's first black president.

Not everyone in this book is as famous as they should be. Yet. Have you heard of **Edith Cavell**? **Sophie Scholl**? **Irena Sendler**? Their wartime stories are truly awe-inspiring.

Martin Luther King Jr. was a wonderful public speaker who made sure that black people's civil rights got the attention they deserved. And **Muhammad Ali** wasn't just the heavyweight boxing champion of the world—he too highlighted the importance of civil rights, as well as refusing to fight in a war that he didn't believe in.

And then there's **Maya Angelou**, who stood up for herself and showed that *anything* is possible.

But whether a slave, a warrior queen, a Tudor superstar, an astronomer, a feminist, a nurse, a president, a leader, an author, a social worker, a student, a civil rights activist, a retired scientist, a cosmologist, a boxing champion, a runner, or a survivor, these people have one thing in common. They didn't sit back and let someone else deal with stuff. They did something about it themselves.

And now for the really cool part. The 25 superstars in this book were not and are not short on experience. So although we don't know exactly what they would say, we tried to imagine what their advice *might* be if they were to tackle some of the tricky problems that you may deal with every day. So along with each life story, you can find out how **Mahatma Gandhi** might tackle bullies or what **Mary Seacole** would say to someone who doubts your ability to do something difficult.

And that's still not everything. At the very end of this book, there's a quiz! Answer the questions to figure out what kind of stander-upper-and-speaker-outer you are.

Remember, you don't have to do any of the jaw-dropping things that our 25 fabulous people have done. They've done them already. You can change the world in a brand-new and totally unique way yourself.

So turn the page, start reading . . . and then make a difference.

SPARTACUS

REBEL GLADIATOR

"I am Spartacus!"
You might have heard someone say this,
swiftly followed by someone else saying,
"I am Spartacus!" You might even have
seen a bunch of Spartacus memes. But what
does the phrase *mean*? Where does it come
from? And who *was* Spartacus anyway?
How did *he* stand up and speak out? To find
out the answers, prepare to travel back over
2,000 years to Roman times, when it was
perfectly acceptable for men to fight to
the death for entertainment.

NAME: *Spartacus*
BORN: circa 109 BC   DIED: 71 BC
NATIONALITY: Thracian
PROFESSION: Gladiator

Historical records from two thousand years ago are sketchy, but it's thought that Spartacus was born in Thrace (now split between Bulgaria, Greece, and Turkey) and may have belonged to the Maedi tribe. He probably became a Roman soldier. Then it's thought that he was captured and sold into slavery. And because he was so strong, he became a gladiator.

Roman gladiators were warriors who fought each other in huge arenas, sometimes to the death (though because it cost so much to train and keep a gladiator, this didn't often happen). Spartacus learned his skills at a gladiatorial school in Capua, near the city of Naples. There were over a hundred of these schools in the Roman Empire.

Roman gladiators were very cool. The public loved them. But that didn't mean they had to be happy to be gladiators. They were still slaves, and they still had to do what the Romans commanded. So, in 73 BC, Spartacus led an escape from gladiator school. He and a number of slaves fled to Mount Vesuvius, where they were joined by many more—enough for Spartacus's own army.

The Romans were worried. They didn't want to be attacked by thousands of highly trained gladiators with a grudge against their captors. So they sent their own soldiers to fight the runaway slaves. Spartacus's army fought back, defeating the Roman attacks again and again. Their rebellion was so effective that it even had its own name—the Third Servile Revolt.

By the time a year had gone by, the Romans had had enough. Roman general Marcus Licinius Crassus led a huge attack on Spartacus, who was finally defeated. Six thousand rebels who escaped the battlefield were later crucified along the Appian Way—a road that led from Rome to Capua.

Spartacus's rebellion inspired many throughout history to fight back against their oppressors. Then, in 1960, the movie *Spartacus* was released. Directed by Stanley Kubrick, it starred Kirk Douglas and Sir Lawrence Olivier.

Spartacus was probably killed in battle. But that wouldn't have made a great ending to the movie. So in it the rebels are told that their lives will be spared if they will identify Spartacus. Before the real Spartacus can speak, the slaves stand and, one by one, they all cry, *"I AM SPARTACUS!"* And because the Romans don't know which of them is telling the truth, they're *all* crucified.

So if Spartacus's name symbolizes rebellion, then the phrase *"I am Spartacus!"* now stands for loyalty. And that's something to shout about.

STAND UP, LIKE SPARTACUS!

Q *It's the hottest heat wave ever. It's not so bad for girls, because they can wear skirts to school. Shorts aren't allowed, though, so the boys have to swelter in pants. In protest, one of them wears a skirt to keep cool in school, to try and change the rules. How do you stand up, like Spartacus?*

A Spartacus would've worn a skirt, too. (To be fair, he'd already have one on because that's what gladiators wore.) But he'd also encourage everyone else to do the same, because he'd know that if people work together, they *can* make a difference.

 # "I AM SPARTACUS."

ANTONIUS,

played by Tony Curtis, and a
crowd of other cast members
of the film *Spartacus* (1960)

BOUDICCA

CELTIC QUEEN

What *was* Boudicca's real name?
It comes from "bouda," the Celtic word
for "victory," but some spell it Boudica.
The Victorians called her Boadicea, but
she is also known as Boudicea, Boadaceia,
and Bunduca. In Wales, she's Buddug!
But whatever she was called, there's no
doubt that she made a name for herself
a thousand years ago in ancient Britain.
It was a time when the Romans were in
charge. Meanwhile, the Britons had been
invaded, and Boudicca was one of many
who really weren't that happy about it.

NAME: *Boudicca*

BORN: circa AD 30   **DIED:** circa AD 60/61

NATIONALITY: British

PROFESSION: Queen

In AD 43, the Romans invaded Britain. (This wasn't a one-time event; it was something they did on a pretty regular basis.) They landed in the south and quickly conquered that part of the country first. Of the many Celtic tribes, most were defeated at once and forced to obey their new rulers. But Prasutagus, king of the Iceni tribe, made a deal with the mighty Romans. If they allowed him to continue to rule alongside the invaders, his lands would be split between his offspring and the Romans when he died. Deal.

Boudicca was Prasutagus's wife—the queen of the Iceni. She was said to be tall and terrifying, with bright red hair and a harsh voice. Basically, you wouldn't want to pick a fight with her. They had two daughters together. The law said that both male and female heirs could inherit, so there wouldn't be a problem after the king's death—the elder daughter would be queen.

But when Prasutagus died in AD 60, the Romans didn't keep their word. Instead of dividing the land fairly, they took it all. Even worse, when Boudicca protested, they beat her and attacked her daughters. The Iceni queen was NOT happy. She wanted revenge. The rest of the Iceni tribe weren't exactly thrilled with the situation either, along with a number of other Celtic tribes. So they all joined together to rebel against the Romans.

Who would lead them? Boudicca, of course. She wasn't going to sit back and let the Romans have it all.

"If you weigh well the strengths of our arms ,you will see that in this battle we must conquer or die," she roared (probably—her words were recorded years later by a Roman historian named Tacitus), before attacking the Roman Ninth Legion. Unsurprisingly, Boudicca and her warriors won.

Next, they headed for Camulodonum. Now called Colchester, this was the capital of Roman Britain. They destroyed it, and thousands died. After this, Boudicca stormed Londinium (which, you might have guessed, is now London). That was destroyed, too. And next stop on the tour of destruction was Verulamium (which is the British city now called St. Albans).

It was Roman general Gaius Suetonius Paulinus—and his army—who put a stop to Boudicca's short-lived reign of terror, which lasted weeks, or possibly months. The Iceni queen may have died in battle, or she may have poisoned herself before the Romans could catch her. Either way, she is famous for standing up to the Roman Empire—the most powerful empire in history.

STAND OUT, LIKE BOUDICCA!

Q *You're so mad. You made a deal with your mom that if you finished all your homework you could stay out later tonight. Now she says that you have to clean your room instead, because it's such a mess. How do you stand up, like Boudicca?*

A Boudicca is perhaps not the best role model here, as she would probably have retaliated by launching a mighty attack and razing your home to the ground. But perhaps a 21st-century Boudicca might have been a little more rational. She'd know that it's not a great idea to fight with parents (especially if your room really is a mess), so she'd clean her room very, very quickly. Then she'd say ever so nicely to your mom that a deal is a deal. So *now* can you go out?

" If you weigh well the strengths of our arms you will see that in this battle we must conquer or die. This is a woman's resolve. As for the men, they may live or be slaves. "

BOUDICCA,
according to Roman historian Tacitus (AD 56–120)

ELIZABETH I

TOP TUDOR

The daughter of Henry VIII and Anne Boleyn, Elizabeth was third in line to the throne and *never* expected to be queen herself. When she was born in the 1500s, kings ruled. End of story. Who knew what would happen to the country if a woman were in charge? And what if a male relative decided he should be monarch instead? There might be war. But when both of Henry's other children died, that left only Elizabeth. Everyone was nervous. Would the new queen be able to stand up for herself *and* her country?

NAME: *Elizabeth I*

BORN: **September 7, 1533**   DIED: **March 24, 1603**

NATIONALITY: **English**

PROFESSION: **Monarch**

Before Elizabeth I was crowned, life in England had been pretty up and down for years. Elizabeth's father, Henry VIII, had married six times, beheading two of his wives, including Elizabeth's own mother. The king had quarreled spectacularly with the Roman Catholic Church—which wouldn't let him divorce—and established the Church of England instead so he could do what he liked. After Henry died, his nine-year-old son, Edward VI, became king and ruled for just six years. Then he too died, and Henry's Roman Catholic daughter, Mary I, took over. She brought back Catholicism and had so many Protestants executed during her five-year reign that she became known as "Bloody Mary." (She almost managed to have Elizabeth herself—her own sister—executed in 1554.) By the time Mary died in 1558 and Elizabeth became queen, everyone was ready for some calm.

The 25-year-old queen's coronation was magnificent. The crowds were huge. In her fabulous clothes, Elizabeth looked and acted like the queen she now was, but she knew the importance of public support, and she didn't forget to speak to those who lined the streets. When the party was over, she got to work.

First, there was the matter of the country's religion to settle. So it was farewell to the Roman Catholic Church (again) and hello to the Church of England (again).

Foreign affairs were tricky. There was a war with France to deal with for a start. Once that was sorted out, there was the constant threat of Spanish invasion. When the Spanish Armada—a fleet of 122 ships—set sail, the danger became real. But when the Spanish ships reached the English Channel, Elizabeth's navy was ready for them. The Armada was defeated (with a little help from the weather).

Meanwhile, there was no shortage of people who wanted to take the throne from the queen. Throughout her reign, plots were uncovered by Elizabeth's spies. She even had Mary Queen of Scots, her own cousin, executed for treason—though she took 19 years to decide whether or not to finish her off. So she clearly didn't rush into things.

But it wasn't all doom and gloom. This was also an age of discovery! Explorer Sir Francis Drake sailed around the world, while Sir Walter Raleigh traveled to North America and set up a colony there.

And what about an heir? The English Parliament was desperate for Elizabeth to marry so that she could produce a child to be the next Tudor monarch. Besides, marriages between royals were such a good way to form alliances between countries. Elizabeth refused. "I am already bound unto a husband, which is the Kingdom of England," she said. When Parliament threatened to cut off her funds, she said sternly that her country was her priority, not her marriage. So there. And she never did marry, though it's said she fell in love.

Elizabeth I was queen for 44 years, until her death in 1603. And as her reign is often known as England's Golden Age, it certainly looks like she was a seriously good queen, too.

STAND UP, LIKE ELIZABETH I!

Q *There's turmoil on the school football team. EVERYONE wants to be captain. You think you're good enough for the job, but how do you make everyone listen? How do you stand out, like Elizabeth I?*

A Elizabeth I was smart. She would know that shouting and screaming is not the way to make everyone listen up. So she would calmly suggest that everyone put forward their plans for leadership. Maybe everyone should try out for the position? After all, being captain is hard. It's important to get the best person for the job.

" I know I have the body of a weak and feeble woman, but I have the heart and stomach of a king, and of a king of England, too.

ELIZABETH I

GALILEO GALILEI

STAR SCIENTIST

The Ancient Greeks thought that Earth was the center of the universe and that the Sun, Moon, planets, and stars orbited it. Centuries later, Polish math whiz Nicolaus Copernicus came up with the theory that it was actually the Sun that was at the center of the universe. But the Catholic Church disagreed. This wasn't what it said in the Bible! So when Galileo Galilei realized that Copernicus was on the right track, he had a choice. Should he ignore his evidence, or should he speak out and risk upsetting the very, very powerful Catholic Church?

NAME: *Galileo Galilei*
BORN: February 15, 1564   DIED: January 8, 1642
NATIONALITY: Italian
PROFESSION: Astronomer, physicist, philosopher, and mathematician

Galileo Galilei was born in Pisa, Italy. He's usually known by his first name, because last names weren't super important in sixteenth-century Italy. (Besides, can you name another Galileo to get him mixed up with?)

Galileo studied medicine at the University of Pisa, where he also became interested in math, physics, astronomy, and philosophy. Unfortunately, he couldn't afford to finish his degree, but he studied math on his own, and four years later he was back at the university. Even better, this time he was teaching.

It was while he was at the University of Pisa that Galileo is famously supposed to have dropped two balls—the same size, but with different masses—from the top of the Leaning Tower of Pisa. He showed that objects accelerate toward Earth at the same rate, regardless of their mass. Many people question whether Galileo actually did the experiment or just thought it. But, either way, he was right.

Next, Galileo moved to the University of Padua. There he lectured crowds of fascinated students and also built his own telescope.

As Galileo watched the night sky through his telescope, he began to believe that Copernicus was right: Earth *did* orbit the Sun. The problem was that the Catholic Church believed that the Sun orbited Earth. When the Church caught wind of Galileo's ideas, they made it illegal to support the Copernican theory. So Galileo kept quiet. As a Catholic, he didn't want to upset the Church.

Seven years later, one of his friends was elected as the pope, and Galileo continued his studies. He wrote a book called *Dialogue Concerning the Two Chief World Systems*. Pope Urban supported this—as long as Galileo included the Copernican theory *and* the Catholic Church's views on how the universe worked, and didn't favor Copernicus.

Oops. Whether he meant to or not, Galileo wrote the book in such a way that it was blindingly obvious that he supported the Copernican theory.

The Catholic Church was furious. Galileo was called to Rome. He was questioned for almost a year and very nearly tortured—at which point he caved in and admitted that he was wrong. The Church was right: Earth was stationary and everything revolved around it. Defiantly, he muttered, *"And yet it moves."* He was, of course, 100% correct. But he spent the rest of his life under house arrest.

It was a whopping 350 years after his death, in 1992, that Pope John Paul II finally admitted that Galileo Galilei was right.

STAND OUT, LIKE GALILEO!

Q *Your teacher has marked off for "mistakes" on your history homework. You're outraged. You've checked your facts and you* know *you're right. But how can you tell a teacher they're wrong? How do you stand up, like Galileo?*

A What do you think? Like you, Galileo would have done the research—he'd know his facts, and he'd be able to back them up. So he'd tell you to gather your evidence and in the politest possible way suggest to your teacher that on this occasion you might be right. What's the worst that could happen? It's not as if your teacher can sentence you to house arrest for the rest of your life.

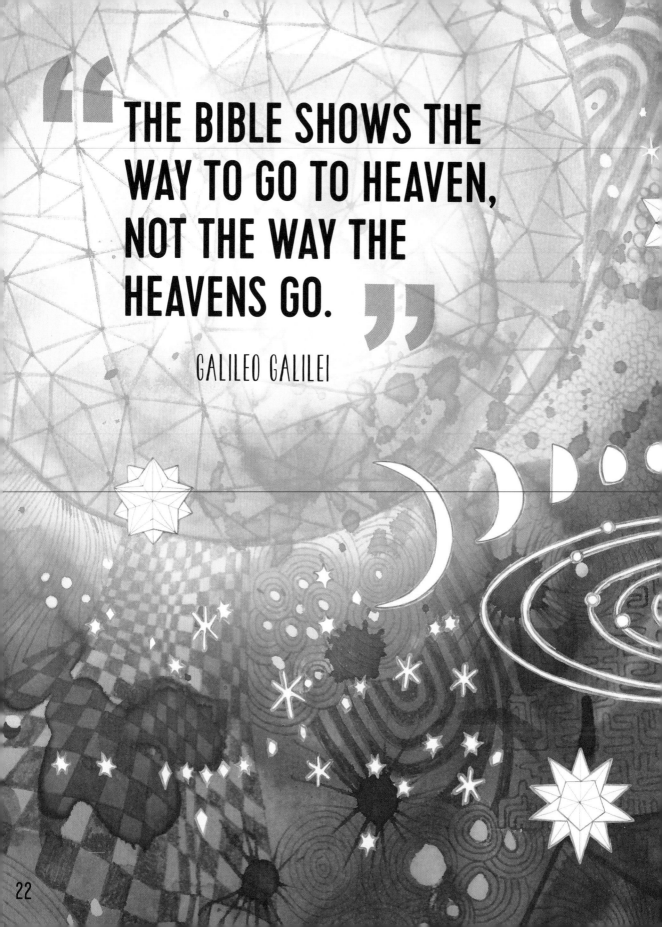

"
THE BIBLE SHOWS THE WAY TO GO TO HEAVEN, NOT THE WAY THE HEAVENS GO.

"

GALILEO GALILEI

MARY WOLLSTONECRAFT

EARLY FEMINIST

Have you heard of Mary Wollstonecraft?
If so, excellent! But if not, don't worry! You're
not alone. She doesn't get anywhere near as
much airtime as other fabulous feminists.
(When she lived, the word "feminist" hadn't
even been invented.) Yet Wollstonecraft
is someone who gave society a good shake
in the 1700s. And she pointed
out that it would be a really good idea if
women had the same rights as men.

NAME: *Mary Wollstonecraft*

BORN: April 27, 1759   DIED: September 10, 1797

NATIONALITY: British

PROFESSION: Author and feminist

It's not surprising that Mary Wollstonecraft had a terrible education. Her father was a violent bully who dragged his family around England and Wales as he tried to make his fortune as a farmer. (He didn't.) She left home as soon as she was old enough, taking a job as a lady's companion.

Next, Wollstonecraft opened a school for girls with her sister and her best friend. It soon ran into financial difficulties and was forced to close. She then worked as a governess in Ireland—and hated it. She especially detested her employer, Lady Kingsborough, whom she thought pretended to be silly and weak in order to get her own way. Unsurprisingly, Wollstonecraft was fired. Afterward, she wrote a short book called *Thoughts on the Education of Daughters*. Many people thought that women didn't need the same level of education as men. Wollstonecraft disagreed. Instead of focusing on manners, she recommended reading. (Hooray!)

In the 1700s, women were often seen as helpless creatures, incapable of thinking for themselves. They were the legal property of their husband or father. Women couldn't own property, and divorce was next to impossible. But it was perfectly fine for a husband to beat his wife. (The law is now very, very different.)

Wollstonecraft's publisher asked her to work on his new magazine—*Analytical Review*. It gave her the chance to meet educated people, read more, and think more. Others looked down their noses at her because she wasn't married, but she didn't care. As far as Wollstonecraft was concerned, it was easier for her to learn than it was for married women. They were far too busy looking beautiful and being supportive wives and mothers, while their husbands had the chance to do all the important thinking themselves. What women needed was a proper education like men, she thought. She wrote about these ideas in a new book called *A Vindication of the Rights of Women*.

After falling in love with an American named Gilbert Imlay, having a baby and—GASP—not marrying him, Wollstonecraft was so worried that society would reject her she pretended they really were husband and wife. She wrote of her sorrow when she and Imlay parted. Philosopher and author William Godwin loved her writing, they met, and she was soon—GASP—pregnant again. This time, she did marry. Many friends were horrified to discover that the first marriage never happened, and her ideas on equality were forgotten. Tragically, Wollstonecraft died just days after giving birth. But her second daughter proved that her mother was right: with a good education, a woman could achieve the same as a man. She was Mary Shelley, the author of *Frankenstein*. And you might have heard of her.

STAND UP, LIKE MARY WOLLSTONECRAFT!

Q "Why do you want to go to college when you're just going to get married and have children?" *your grandfather says to you. How do you reply to that?! How do you stand up, like Mary Wollstonecraft?*

A Once she'd picked her jaw up off the floor, Mary Wollstonecraft would tell your grandfather that everyone deserves a good education, regardless of whether they're a boy or a girl. How else are they supposed to have the same chances in life? Then she would very politely remind your grandfather that it's the 21st century. And then she would run and hide until he recovers from the shock.

> " Let woman share the rights, and she will emulate the virtues of man. "

MARY WOLLSTONECRAFT

MARY SEACOLE

STAR NURSE

When it comes to star nurses of the Crimean War, Florence Nightingale is the one who always gets top billing. But she wasn't the only nurse to brave terrible conditions in order to treat injured soldiers. There's also Mary Seacole. She was a Jamaican nurse who tried to join Nightingale and her team, but she was turned down. Did she give up? Nope. She simply found a different way to get there.

NAME: **Mary Jane Seacole**

BORN: **November 23, 1805**   DIED: **May 14, 1881**

NATIONALITY: **British-Jamaican**

PROFESSION: **Nurse**

Mary Seacole was from Kingston, Jamaica. Her father was a Scottish soldier, and her mother a Jamaican nurse and traditional healer who taught Seacole all her skills. She also ran a boardinghouse for sick and injured soldiers, which was an excellent place to pick up medical tips from army doctors.

If there was one thing Seacole loved, it was traveling. She went to London—twice—and also sailed to the Bahamas, Haiti, and Cuba, finding out about different medical treatments and medicines on the way. She was married briefly, but after her husband died, she focused on nursing, going to Panama to care for patients during a cholera epidemic. (For the record, this was a very brave thing to do. Cholera is a deadly disease.) Then she returned to Jamaica to care for victims of yellow fever (which was no laughing matter either). On her travels she had gained a huge amount of practical medical experience.

Then war broke out between Great Britain and the Russian Empire in the Crimea—a peninsula in the Black Sea. Immediately, Seacole decided to help. She traveled to Great Britain, where Florence Nightingale was gathering a team of nurses to take to the Crimea. This was excellent timing! Now Seacole could go, too, and help treat the many soldiers injured in this terrible war. So she volunteered at once but the government turned her down, along with two other black women. Seacole was convinced it was because of the color of their skin. When Nightingale set sail with 38 nurses, Seacole wasn't one of them.

It didn't matter, though. Seacole went anyway. She borrowed money from a friend named Thomas Day, and they stocked up with supplies and set sail together for the Crimea. Seacole was going not as an official nurse, but as a sutler—this was a person who followed an army and sold provisions. At this time, the army didn't take care of its soldiers.

Nightingale and her nurses were treating sick and injured soldiers in a hospital in Scutari, Turkey. This was actually around 300 miles away from the battlefields. On their way to the battlefront, Seacole and Day visited Scutari where they met Nightingale. Seacole wrote in her memoirs that Nightingale was very nice to her and offered her help.

But Seacole and Day didn't stay in Scutari. They traveled on and set up the British Hotel near Balaclava, where the fighting was actually happening. (The British Hotel wasn't a real hotel, by the way. It was a metal hut. But the soldiers obviously weren't picky.) As well as selling food, drink, and clothes to the soldiers, Seacole nursed them. She also witnessed the Battle of Sebastapol, treating wounded soldiers on the battlefield. She became known as Mother Seacole.

When she returned to Great Britain after the war, Seacole was penniless and ill. But her story was highlighted in the newspapers, and people were so impressed with her bravery that they raised money to support her. She went on to write *The Wonderful Adventures of Mary Seacole in Many Lands*. These adventures never would have happened if she'd stayed at home.

STAND OUT, LIKE MARY SEACOLE!

Q *You're pretty sure that it doesn't take a rocket scientist to change a bike chain, and you'd like to give it a try. But your dad doesn't think you can do it. He's threatening to take it to the bike repair shop instead. How do you stand up, like Mary Seacole?*

A Mary Seacole wasn't a trained nurse—in fact, there wasn't really any official nursing training in her day—but by learning whenever and wherever she could, she managed to make a lot of people feel better. So she might suggest that you research the topic until you know it inside out. Then try to persuade your dad. And if he still won't let you change the bike chain, go to the repair shop and watch it being done. Then *you* can work some mechanical magic next time.

> And the grateful words and smile which rewarded me for binding up a wound or giving a cooling drink was a pleasure worth risking life for at any time.

MARY SEACOLE

ABRAHAM LINCOLN

PRESIDENT OF THE FREE

Can you name every single one of the United States presidents? If so, WOW. You should consider running for president yourself. If not, don't worry. Neither can most other people. But there is one name that stands head and shoulders above the rest. And it's not just because this president also happened to be the tallest president. (And wore a very tall hat.) Abraham Lincoln is widely regarded to be one of the greatest presidents of all time, if not *the* greatest. But why?

NAME: *Abraham Lincoln*

BORN: February 12, 1809   DIED: April 15, 1865

NATIONALITY: American

PROFESSION: President of the United States

Abraham Lincoln didn't go to a fancy school or college. When he was born, his pioneer family lived in a log cabin in Kentucky. Life was hard. They were very poor, so school was out of the question. Instead, Lincoln had to work to help support the family. Determined to make something of himself, he wanted to learn. His stepmother encouraged him to read, and he loved it. So although he only briefly went to school, Lincoln used books to teach himself.

After leaving home, Lincoln moved to New Salem, Illinois. He quickly made friends, earning a reputation for being funny and smart. He dived into politics for the first time and became a member of the Whig Party. Then he studied law—again, he was self-taught—and passed the bar examination. (You didn't need to go to law school to become a lawyer in those days.) He was a good one, too; his clients called him "Honest Abe." Then it was back to politics, in which he was the only Whig to win a seat in the United States House of Representatives. (This is one of the two houses that make up the United States Congress; the other is the Senate.) When Lincoln spoke out against slavery, the Whigs didn't like it, and he eventually left.

He joined the brand-new Republican Party! It opposed slavery, something that was very important to Lincoln. Slavery was also an issue that was growing increasingly important to the rest of the country. The southern states wanted to keep their slaves, while the northern states wanted slavery to be banned. "A house divided against itself cannot stand," said Lincoln, who was now campaigning for a seat in the Senate. He lost. But that didn't matter, because his party now thought he was so fabulous they chose him as their presidential candidate. And he won! Abraham Lincoln became the sixteenth president of the United States.

Then seven southern slave states left the Union and formed the Confederacy. This meant war: the American Civil War. Lincoln took charge. To begin with, he said that he wanted to bring all the states back together into one nation. But because the main argument was really the abolition of slavery, he later shifted the focus. In his Emancipation Proclamation, he declared that slaves in all of the rebellious states were "forever free." Now it was a war for freedom. Lincoln's famous Gettysburg Address underlined this—*"all men are created equal,"* said the president.

The Civil War lasted four long, brutal years. At last, the Union won. But hundreds of thousands of soldiers were dead, and six days later, so was Lincoln. A month before the war ended, he was assassinated at a theater by John Wilkes Booth—a big fan of the Confederates.

But Lincoln's legacy was huge. Millions of slaves were free, at last.

"Whatever you are, be a good one."

ABRAHAM LINCOLN

STAND UP, LIKE ABE LINCOLN!

Q *A so-called best friend did something unforgiveable. (It's too unforgiveable even to write.) They've apologized, but you can't forget what they did. You don't think you'll EVER be able to treat them the same way again. How do you forgive, like Abe?*

A You might be surprised to learn that even after the horrors of the Civil War, when asked by a general how to deal with the losing side, Abraham Lincoln told him to go easy. So even though your friend did a really bad thing, they did say sorry. Best friends don't come along every day. It would be really sad to lose one, right?

EDITH CAVELL

NURSING HERO

Edith Cavell was a nurse—a really good one. But that's not all. During the First World War, she was also involved with a spy network that, in addition to helping wounded soldiers escape wartime Belgium, also sent back secret intelligence to the Allies. It was a risky thing to do. And she paid a very heavy price for her bravery.

NAME: *Edith Louisa Cavell*
BORN: December 4, 1865 DIED: October 12, 1915
NATIONALITY: British
PROFESSION: Nurse

Edith Cavell had an unremarkable childhood. She grew up in a pretty English village where her father was a priest. She went to school locally, and then to boarding school. And then she worked as a governess in Brussels, Belgium. But when Cavell's father became ill, she returned home to care for him. He recovered —yay!—and she decided that nursing was the career for her. She trained hard and must have been a pretty fabulous nurse, because in 1907 she was chosen to lead a brand-new nursing school back in Brussels. So off she went.

By 1914, war was looming. Eager to avoid fighting on the Russian and French borders at the same time, the Germans decided to follow the ever-so-clever (so they thought) Schlieffen Plan. Part of this plan involved storming through Belgium and surprising the French army from the north.

When the First World War broke out, Cavell was visiting her mother in England. She was nowhere near the fighting. But when she heard about the invasion of Belgium, she whizzed back to Brussels at once. That was where she was needed. Cavell's nursing school was turned into a Red Cross hospital. And it didn't matter which side they were on—all were treated there.

Belgium was now under enemy occupation. But even though Allies sent to defend the country had now been forced back, an awful lot of soldiers had been left behind. How were *they* supposed to escape?

Slowly, an underground network of safe houses was created. Soldiers and fugitives were secretly passed from one place to another until they could reach freedom. When two wounded British soldiers were sent to Cavell, she gave them beds at the hospital before sending them toward the Netherlands. This was a risky thing to do. If caught, the punishment was death. Nevertheless, Cavell ignored the danger and went on to help as many as 200 people escape, until she was arrested, imprisoned and found guilty of treason. She was executed by firing squad.

A hundred years later, it's suspected that Cavell was actually working for the British intelligence services. As well as smuggling people, the network was also a way of communicating top-secret information about the enemy. But whether she was an actual spy or not makes little difference. Cavell stood up to the enemy, and she saved a lot of people on the way.

STAND OUT, LIKE EDITH CAVELL!

Q *Your best friends have argued, BIG TIME. You don't know what to do. If you speak to either one of them, the other is going to be mad. But one has invited you to a birthday party, while the other wants you to go shopping. How do you stand up, like Edith Cavell?*

A It's difficult when you're stuck in the middle of fighting friends. But Edith Cavell treated *all* soldiers during the First World War, regardless of which side they were on. So, like her, try to treat your friends the same and see both of them. Don't keep it a secret, though. Let each of them know that you're not letting a silly fight get in the way of a perfectly fab friendship, and perhaps they'll soon work out their differences.

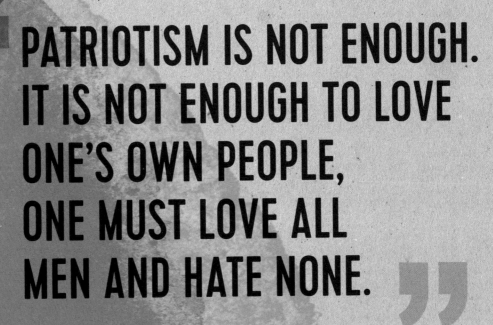

"PATRIOTISM IS NOT ENOUGH.
IT IS NOT ENOUGH TO LOVE
ONE'S OWN PEOPLE,
ONE MUST LOVE ALL
MEN AND HATE NONE."

EDITH CAVELL

MAHATMA GANDHI

GREAT SOUL

Gandhi wasn't called Mahatma to begin with. It means "great soul," and was a name given to him after he used non violent civil disobedience as a way to make a difference. Also unofficially known in India as the Father of the Nation, Gandhi became so famous worldwide that he was named *Time* magazine's "Man of the Year" in 1930. He showed us that violence doesn't have to be the answer.

NAME: *Mahatma Mohandas Karamchand Gandhi*

BORN: October 2, 1869   DIED: January 30, 1948

NATIONALITY: Indian

PROFESSION: Leader of non violent independence movement

Gandhi was lucky. His father had a great job—he was the chief minister of Porbandar in Gujarat—which meant that his family didn't have to worry about being poor, unlike so many others in India. Gandhi's family was Hindu, and his mother was super religious. She taught Gandhi to be vegetarian, to be tolerant of others, and never to be violent.

He wasn't the world's best student. And after an arranged marriage at the age of 13—yes, really—Gandhi became a rebellious teenager. He wasn't any happier at a university in Bombay. So when he was given the chance to study law in London, he went for it. London proved to be the perfect place for Gandhi to return to his Hindu roots, and for him to study the world's religions. He also passed his law exams.

After a short, unsuccessful spell as a lawyer in India, Gandhi and his family moved to South Africa for a fresh start. Here, he was horrified to be thrown out of a first-class train car because of his skin color. Gandhi decided that he needed to change things. So he set up the Natal Indian Congress to fight against segregation in South Africa. Except this would be a fight with a difference—it would be peaceful. He called his campaign Satyagraha, meaning "truth and firmness."

For 21 years, Gandhi protested against the South African government's unfair laws. He organized strikes and marches. He and his followers allowed themselves to be arrested. Gandhi became so effective at non violent civil disobedience that when he left South Africa in 1914, one politician wrote that he hoped Gandhi would be gone forever.

Meanwhile, India had been under British rule since 1858. Gandhi had always supported the British. But after the Massacre of Amritsar in 1919, when British troops killed hundreds of Indians, he changed his mind. He believed that Indians should rule themselves. So he kick-started a new campaign, asking his people to stop working for the British, stop going to British schools, stop paying taxes, and stop buying British goods. He even made his own clothes (a traditional Indian white garment called a dhoti), rather than buying from the British.

As the leader of the Indian National Congress, Gandhi led thousands of Indians across the country in 1930 to protest against Britain's unfair Salt Acts. These prevented Indians from collecting or selling salt, and made them buy expensive British salt. Gandhi was jailed, and the law was changed, but British rule remained. When the British prime minister Winston Churchill asked India to fight in the Second World War, Ghandi told the British to "quit India" instead.

In 1947, India was finally given its independence from Britain, though Partition meant that the country was split in two because of religious differences. It became India and Pakistan. Violence erupted. Although he had achieved so much, Gandhi's dream of a peaceful India had not yet been achieved.

Tragically, after spending his life promoting peace, Mahatma Gandhi was assassinated by a religious extremist. Almost one million people came to watch his funeral procession. But this was a fraction of the number of people who mourned him worldwide.

STAND UP, LIKE GANDHI!

Q *A gang of bullies is threatening to attack you and your friends on the playground. They're bigger, stronger, and much scarier than you. How can you possibly fight back? How do you stand up, like Gandhi?*

A Gandhi would know that he didn't need to fight back. And he'd also know that a lot of people can make a difference if they stick together. So he would start a campaign of non violence to thwart the bullies. He would get his friends together and attack the bullies with a barrage of hard stares. He would annoy the bullies by refusing to be scared of their threats. (He'd probably tell the teachers what was going on, too, because teachers are pretty good at dealing with this kind of thing.) The very last thing that Gandhi would do would be to fight back. Because he knew that you don't have to fight to win.

" Non violence is the greatest force at the disposal of mankind. It is mightier than the mightiest weapon of destruction. "

MAHATMA GANDHI

HELEN KELLER

INSPIRATIONAL SPEAKER

When it comes to inspirational people, Helen Keller is right up there. She lost her sight *and* her hearing before she was two, yet went on to communicate, study, write, and champion the rights of others. As one of the founders of the American Civil Liberties Union, her legacy is an organization that protects the rights of all Americans—from LGBT equality to the right to vote. Basically, she rocked.

NAME: *Helen Adams Keller*

BORN: June 27, 1880   DIED: June 1, 1968

NATIONALITY: American

PROFESSION: Author and political activist

Whether she caught scarlet fever or meningitis, no one knows, but by the age of 19 months, Keller was blind and deaf. Amazingly, she still managed to communicate. She and the family cook's daughter developed their own form of sign language. But Keller's behavior swung between extremes—she was so uncontrollable that relatives suggested she should be sent to an institution.

Instead, Keller's mother tried to find other ways to help her daughter and was put in touch with Alexander Graham Bell, whose mother and wife were both deaf, and who taught deaf children to speak. (This is the same Alexander Graham Bell who invented the telephone.) Bell—who remained a lifelong friend of Keller's—recommended the Perkins School for the Blind in Boston. They suggested that a former pupil named Anne Sullivan might be able to help. Sullivan soon moved into the Keller home, and the lessons began.

Things didn't go well at first. Keller was angry, frustrated, and uncooperative. But Sullivan kept going, trying to help Keller make connections between objects and their names, spelling letters out in her student's hand. Finally, Sullivan poured water over Keller's hand and then spelled out the word "water." At once, Keller spelled the letters back to her teacher. It was a huge breakthrough. Her vocabulary soon grew.

Next, she learned how to speak. School followed. Keller met Mark Twain—the author of *Huckleberry Finn*—who was seriously impressed with her efforts to communicate. A rich friend of his met Keller, too, and then paid for her to continue her education. This was a wonderful development. Keller desperately wanted to go to college, and now she could! Sullivan went, too, accompanying her old student to lectures so that she could communicate to Keller what she could neither see nor hear. It was a huge success. Keller became the first deaf and blind person to be awarded a degree.

Now Helen Keller stepped it up a gear. She'd achieved so much that she wanted to help others do the same. As well as writing her autobiography—*The Story of My Life*—and many other books, she wrote magazine articles explaining to readers what it meant to be blind. She traveled around the world giving lectures on behalf of the American Foundation for the Blind.

She became an ambassador for Helen Keller International, which is still going strong over a hundred years later. The charity works to improve the sight and lives of the world's poor, while helping children living with blindness in Africa and Asia get a good education. She was one of the founding members of the American Civil Liberties Union, standing up for civil rights. Meanwhile, she campaigned for women's rights and suffrage—the right to vote.

Helen Keller couldn't see or hear. But that didn't stop her from speaking out.

STAND OUT, LIKE HELEN KELLER!

Q *You're terribly, terribly shy. So when your school asks for volunteers to take part in a debate competition, you say no right away—even though you'd really love to be involved. How do you stand out, like Helen Keller?*

A You know what's coming, right? Helen Keller (and pretty much every other person featured in this book, and your parents, and your best friend) would tell you to do it. Go for it. You're shy? No one will ever guess. Take a deep breath and give it a try. You might even enjoy it.

> The only thing worse than being blind is having sight but no vision.
>
> HELEN KELLER

GEORGE ORWELL

VIBRANT VISIONARY

If there was one thing George Orwell wasn't short of, it was opinions. He didn't actually stand up and speak out about them, though. He wrote wonderful books instead. His writing made such a big impression that an adjective was named after him. If something is Orwellian, it means that it's like the dark, scary future Orwell wrote about in *Nineteen Eighty-Four*. And if you'd like your own adjective, be prepared to do something really memorable. Like George Orwell.

NAME: *Eric Arthur Blair*

BORN: June 25, 1903   DIED: January 21, 1950
NATIONALITY: British   PROFESSION: Author

Eric Arthur Blair was born in India. (If you're wondering what Eric Arthur Blair has to do with anything, that was George Orwell's real name.) At this time, the British ruled India, and his father worked for the civil service there. When he was very young, however, Blair moved back to England with his mother and sister.

Blair's parents liked to think they were refined, but even though they both came from well-off families, there was one thing they didn't have: money. When it became clear that their son was super smart, they wanted him to go to a top notch school, but they couldn't afford it. Luckily, the problem was solved when Blair won a scholarship to a boarding school, and another and another. By the time he was a teenager, Blair was at Eton College—a very famous British school.

Blair then moved to Burma (now Myanmar), where he worked for the India Imperial Police. Slowly, he realized how much the Burmese hated being ruled by the British, and he felt guilty being a part of such a system. So he quit, ready to begin a completely different career. He was going to be a writer. To do this, he chose a new name: George Orwell, probably because of the River Orwell near his parents' home in Southwold, Suffolk.

Writing wasn't a new thing. It was something Orwell had always loved. But he needed to earn money to support himself while he wrote. In London and then Paris, he had a string of badly paid jobs and found out what it was really like to be poor in those cities. A friend had advised him to write about what he knew about, so he did. He wrote *Down and Out in Paris and London*.

Next, he wrote *Burmese Days*—a novel based on his time in Burma. In *The Road to Wigan Pier*, he described the terrible poverty suffered by unemployed miners in northern England in the 1930s, after visiting the area.

Next, Orwell took part in the Spanish Civil War (1936-1939). He fought on the side of the Republicans—supported by Stalin, the communist Soviet leader—against General Franco and his Nationalist forces. Franco won and took control. Meanwhile, Orwell was badly injured. He fled the country with a great dislike for communism and especially Stalin. Orwell felt that the Soviet leader had manipulated the war for his country's own benefit. So it's no surprise that he wrote *Animal Farm*.

Animal Farm appears to be the story of farmyard animals who rebel against their human masters so they can live freely (until things start to go horribly wrong). But it is actually Orwell's clever retelling of the Russian Revolution of 1917. The book was a huge success. Orwell became very famous.

The year 1984 is now very last century. But when Orwell's *Nineteen Eighty-Four* was published, it was still in the future. And it was a very bleak, sinister future indeed. In *Nineteen Eighty-Four*, everyone is watched, all of the time. There is no free speech. The government controls everything. The problem is, the main character wants to think for himself.

Nineteen Eighty-Four was Orwell's last book. He was ill when he wrote it and died just months after it was published. But the book and its ideas remain very, very important today. Like Orwell.

> ## If liberty means anything at all, it means the right to tell people what they do not want to hear.

GEORGE ORWELL

STAND UP, LIKE GEORGE ORWELL!

Q *You feel like you're living in a real-life version of* Nineteen Eighty-Four. *It's like Big Brother is watching you ALL THE TIME. You're told when to get up, when to go to bed, when to do homework, everything! What would George Orwell do?*

A Did you know that the term "Big Brother" actually comes from *Nineteen Eighty-Four*? You do now. (So does the expression "Room 101.") There's a chance Orwell would tell you to fight back against the establishment, but he'd also know that parents aren't really totalitarian governments. So he might suggest that you do all your homework without them having to nag you about it. Try getting up before they call you. Go to bed before they harp on about that, too. And then they might actually realize that it's time to give you more freedom.

IRENA SENDLER

SAVIOR OF CHILDREN

The Holocaust was the worst genocide
in history. Six million Jews were
systematically murdered by Hitler
and the Nazis, just for being Jewish.
There were many, many people who
risked their lives to save the Jews.
Perhaps this is the first you've heard of
Irena Sendler, but for a Jewish child in
Poland during the Second World War,
she might well have been the most
important person in their life.

NAME: *Irena Sendler*

BORN: February 15, 1910   DIED: May 12, 2008

NATIONALITY: Polish

PROFESSION: Social worker

At the beginning of the war, Sendler was living in Warsaw, Poland, where she was employed as a social worker. She was in charge of "canteens" in the Polish capital—these provided food and aid for those in need. When Poland was invaded in 1939 and war began, Sendler made sure that the canteens helped the country's Jews.

To say that the Nazis didn't like the Jews is a massive understatement. They thought Jews were inferior—along with many other groups of people. Horrifyingly, they tried to get rid of them all. More than 3 million Jews lived in Poland at the time, and the Nazis decided to move them all to areas called ghettos. These weren't nice places to live—they were actually prisons, surrounded by brick walls and barbed wire. Anyone who tried to escape risked being shot by armed guards.

The Warsaw Ghetto was the biggest of them all. More than a third of a million Jews were forced to live in an area the size of Central Park in New York City. From here, Jewish people were sent to Nazi concentration camps and almost certain death. Conditions in the ghetto were terrible. It was crowded and dirty. There was little food and not enough medical supplies. Many people became ill and died.

And that's where Sendler came in. Her job as a social worker meant that she was one of the few non-Jewish people able to get into the ghetto. She obtained a permit to enter the ghetto so that she could inspect the conditions there. But once she was inside, she made contact with the Jews instead. She told them that she wanted to help them escape.

Sendler became a member of a group called Żegota, which was formed to help Jews. She was in charge of smuggling children out of the ghetto. This wasn't easy. Sendler had to use increasingly ingenious ways to help them escape. Sometimes, children hid inside the few ambulances that *were* allowed inside the ghetto, or they pretended to be so ill that they needed to go to the hospital. They crawled along sewer pipes and underground passages. They hid in sacks, trunks and suitcases. Sendler did whatever she could to get them out. Then she found families and convents where the children could hide until the war was over.

In 1943, disaster struck when Sendler was arrested by the Nazis. They tortured her so that she would tell them who she was working with. When she refused, they sentenced her to death. But Żegota members bribed the prison guards, and she was freed! She went straight back to leading children to safety. And she lived until the ripe old age of 98. By the end of the war, Sendler had saved 400 children's lives.

> # "Fear makes you weak; anger makes you strong."

IRENA SENDLER

STAND OUT, LIKE IRENA SENDLER!

Q *You've seen some terrible stories on the news about children suffering in a war zone far away. You want to help, but you don't know how. How do you stand up, like Irena Sendler?*

A If Irena Sendler wasn't old enough to go and help in person, she would probably have tried to help from home. She might begin by raising awareness for the children's plight. Or she might find out which charities were involved and raise money to help *them* help the children.

55

NELSON MANDELA

THE FATHER OF THE NATION

With a name like "troublemaker"—that really *is* what Rolihlahla means in the Xhosa language—it's perhaps no surprise that Nelson Mandela wasn't afraid to make a stir. What is astonishing is how much of a stir he made. Mandela refused to put up with his country's deeply unfair apartheid system. So he became an anti-apartheid activist. No one dreamed where this would take him and South Africa.

NAME: **Nelson Rolihlahla Mandela**

BORN: July 18, 1918 DIED: December 5, 2013

NATIONALITY: **South African**

PROFESSION: **President of South Africa**

Rolihlahla Mandela was born in a small village in South Africa. The great-grandson of the king of the Thembu tribe, he was the first person in his family to go to school. His teacher named him Nelson—a throwback to the colonizers, who found African names too difficult to pronounce.

By the time he was in college, Mandela was already in trouble—he was expelled for taking part in a student protest. But it wasn't until a few years later that he became really political and joined the African National Congress (ANC). Its aim was to bring African people together at a time when black and white people were kept apart. (*Apartheid* actually means "apartness.") Mandela helped form the brand new ANC Youth League, to involve young people in the struggle. He soon became its president.

Under the government's apartheid law, South Africans did everything separately, according to the color of their skin. They used different parks, buses, train cars, taxis, toilets, water fountains, and so many more things that there isn't room to list them here. People of different races couldn't marry each other. They went to different schools and were forced to live in different areas. There are no prizes for guessing that living conditions in black peoples' townships were terrible. And there was no way that nonwhites could elect a new government, because they couldn't vote either.

The ANC organized boycotts and strikes against apartheid, but it soon became clear that peaceful protests weren't having any effect. What's more, Mandela was regularly being arrested and put in jail, so it was becoming impossible for him to speak out at rallies. When police killed 69 people and injured many more during a peaceful demonstration in Sharpeville on March 21, 1960, violence erupted. Thousands were arrested—Mandela too—and the ANC was banned.

Mandela kept a low profile, leaving the country illegally to gather support for the ANC's activities. But as soon as he got back, he was arrested yet again, and this time it was serious. Found guilty of leaving South Africa without a passport and for encouraging strikes, he was sent to prison for five years. This wasn't any old prison. This was Robben Island—a maximum-security prison off the coast of Cape Town. When seven other ANC members—and Mandela—were found guilty of sabotage, they were all sentenced to life imprisonment, with hard labor. Mandela wasn't going to be freed any time soon.

In fact, Mandela was imprisoned for 27 years. He could have gotten out sooner. President P. W. Botha offered three times to release him on condition that he renounce violence. Mandela refused. It was only after President F. W. de Klerk was elected and started banishing apartheid that Mandela was finally freed, unconditionally. South Africa and the rest of the world went wild.

Mandela and President de Klerk shared the Nobel Peace Prize in 1993, and a year later—as the president of the ANC once more—Mandela became South Africa's first black president in an election where *everyone* voted.

> ❝ Education is the most powerful weapon which you can use to change the world. ❞
>
> NELSON MANDELA

STAND UP, LIKE NELSON MANDELA!

Q *You're so excited. You've been practicing basketball nonstop and you'd love to try out for the school team. But the coach isn't interested. "I already have the best team," he says. "There's no way you're good enough." How do you stand out, like Mandela?*

A *Ahem.* There's no need to be exactly like Mandela, of course. Twenty-seven years is an awfully long time to be imprisoned. (Being prepared to die for your cause is a little extreme, too.) But if you think something is unfair, then stand up for what you believe in. And even if the coach says that you can try out next year, don't give in. Mandela didn't.

SOPHIE SCHOLL

REBEL STUDENT

You might not have heard of Sophie Scholl. She's not particularly famous outside of Germany, but she should be. Sophie was a member of the White Rose—a resistance group of college students and a professor who stood up to the Nazis during the Second World War. The White Rose members weren't violent. But they didn't need weapons. They were using something much more powerful—words.

In the early 1930s, Germany was in the doldrums. Still reeling from its defeat in the First World War and still paying back huge amounts of compensation demanded by the Allies after the war, the country was in the middle of an economic depression. Prices skyrocketed daily, and millions were unemployed. The government was struggling to cope. So when the Nationalist Socialist German Workers' Party—the Nazis, for short—came into power, many were delighted. Perhaps they would make Germany prosperous again.

Sophie Scholl's parents weren't so sure about the new government and its leader, Adolf Hitler. But, at first, Sophie (she was named Sophia but known as Sophie) didn't have a problem with the Nazis, and neither did her brother Hans. Along with thousands of other young Germans, Hans joined the Hitler Youth, while Sophie became a member of the League of German Girls. Both organizations supported Nazi ideals: promoting a strong, independent Germany; uniting German speakers; and stopping immigration.

But as time went on, the Nazis grew more extreme. It became illegal to form a new political party to challenge the government. Hitler was no longer a leader; he was a dictator. "Un-German" books were burned in huge bonfires. New laws were passed that discriminated against Jews, and Sophie's Jewish friends were prevented from joining the League of German Girls. Sophie became totally disillusioned. From now on, she wouldn't support the Nazis. She would fight against them.

Her big chance came in 1942. The Second World War was happening, and Nazi propaganda was everywhere. Now a college student, Sophie found a leaflet that spoke out *against* the Nazis. This was a seriously dangerous thing to do. Anyone discovered criticizing the Nazis could be killed. Anyone who didn't report such a thing was in trouble, too, but she pocketed the leaflet anyway. She wanted to find out who was responsible. She wanted to help them.

Sophie couldn't believe it when she discovered that Hans—her own brother—was involved. He and other students were part of a resistance group called the White Rose. The group wrote anti-Nazi and anti-war leaflets. Then they secretly distributed thousands of copies to other Germans. Now the White Rose had another member—Sophie Scholl.

In February 1943, Sophie and Hans Scholl distributed copies of the White Rose's sixth and final leaflet at the University of Munich. They left them everywhere—in classrooms, hallways, and on windowsills. It's said that Sophie pushed the final pile of leaflets from a balcony, so they tumbled like confetti onto the students below. They were seen and caught. They were interrogated, and sentenced to death for high treason. And then they were executed.

The names of Sophie and her brother Hans appear on schools throughout Germany. But the most powerful memorial is the White Rose Pavement Memorial. The scattered bronze leaflets set among the cobblestones of a Munich square is a poignant reminder of the bravery of the Scholl siblings and the other members of the White Rose.

> "Stand up for what you believe in, even if you are standing alone."
>
> SOPHIE SCHOLL

STAND OUT, LIKE SOPHIE SCHOLL!

 A developer wants to close your town's library and turn the building into fancy apartments. They're on the verge of getting city permission. The situation is desperate. The library might close! How do you stand up, like Sophie Scholl?

 The White Rose wrote leaflets that blew the Nazis' cover. They told people what was really going on. They spoke from the heart and tried to convince people to join the resistance. You can do it, too! (And as you're not going to have to borrow money to buy a printing press, it's going to be a whole lot easier.) Tell everyone what's going on, any way you can. Write leaflets and hand them out at the library door. Get on social media. Phone the local radio station. E-mail the newspapers. Do whatever you can to spread the word, and you just might make a difference.

MAYA ANGELOU

UTTERLY UNIQUE

Who *was* Maya Angelou?
A civil rights activist? A poet?
An author? A composer? An actor?
A director? A professor? A streetcar
conductor? Unbelievably, Angelou was
all of these things—and even more. Her
life was anything but easy, but that didn't
keep her from excelling at one thing
after another. So perhaps the best way to
describe her is as an all-singing,
all-dancing superstar. (And, yes, she was
a singer and a dancer, too.)

NAME: *Marguerite Annie Johnson Angelou*

BORN: April 4, 1928   DIED: May 28, 2014

NATIONALITY: American

PROFESSION: You name it, Maya Angelou probably did it!

Maya Angelou's childhood was tough. Her parents got divorced when she was three, and she and her brother were raised by her grandmother in Arkansas. She was abused by her mother's boyfriend, who was then murdered. Blaming herself for his death, Angelou stopped speaking—for five years. While she was silent, Angelou read and read and developed a love of words. At last, a kind teacher named Bertha Flowers helped her speak again.

Angelou went to high school in San Francisco, where she won a scholarship to study dance and drama. Then at age 17, she had a baby. As a single mother, she now had to support herself and her son, so she worked as a streetcar conductor, a dancer, and a cook to make ends meet. She later married, but separated. Then, she was spotted by a talent scout and joined the cast of *Porgy and Bess*. The Gershwin opera—which starred African-American singers and was set in South Carolina—toured Europe. Next, she wrote and recorded her first album.

Meanwhile, black and white people still weren't being treated equally. Angelou was very, very angry about this until she heard Martin Luther King Jr. speak about the black civil rights movement. At last! Here was something that she could become involved with. So she joined King's movement, organizing a fundraising event named *Cabaret for Freedom* to support his work. When she later met Malcolm X—another famous civil rights activist—she worked with him, too. When Malcom X and then King were assassinated, she was devastated. Angelou's friends rallied around. They'd heard the stories of her life, and thought they needed to be told. So with their encouragement, she wrote the first of her seven autobiographies.

I Know Why the Caged Bird Sings tells the story of Angelou's troubled childhood and how she was affected by prejudice, racism, sexism, and segregation. It tells how Angelou's employer changed her name from Marguerite to Mary, because it was easier to say. It tells how the Ku Klux Klan—a racist organization—terrorized her neighborhood and how a white dentist refused to treat her because she was black. But the book also tells how she fought back, striking a chord with readers—both those who'd suffered from the same issues as Angelou and those who had no idea such unacceptable things happened. It was an instant hit, nominated for the National Book Award.

Success followed success. Angelou excelled at poetry, screenwriting, acting, composing, and essays. She worked on two presidential committees. She was given honorary degrees and awards by the dozen, including the prestigious Literarian Award, the Presidential Medal of Arts, and the Presidential Medal of Freedom.

But despite the many accolades, perhaps she is most famous for making people understand what it was really like for a black girl to grow up in the Deep South—and urging them to do something about it.

> " If you don't like something, change it. If you can't change it, change your attitude. "
>
> MAYA ANGELOU

STAND UP, LIKE MAYA ANGELOU!

Q *You've interviewed the oldest members of your family, and it turns out that there are some seriously cool stories just waiting to be told. But how? How do you stand out, like Maya Angelou?*

A Angelou was never trapped by a single medium—she used *all* of them. So while she'd be totally on board with a riveting biography, she'd also consider transforming a family history into poetry, a school play, a song, or modern dance. Or maybe she'd use a whizzy app to make a movie about it—and then star in it, too. Whatever you choose, just go for it. Angelou would.

MARTIN LUTHER KING JR.

DREAMER

Martin Luther King Jr. had a dream.
He dreamed that all people would be equal.
The problem was, while he was growing up in
Georgia, black and white people were treated
differently because of the color of their skin.
They were segregated, or kept apart. And
marriage between people of different races was
strictly against the law. Martin Luther King Jr.
wanted to change all that. But how would he
make his dream come true?

BORN: January 15, 1929   DIED: April 4, 1968
NATIONALITY: **American**
PROFESSION: **Baptist minister and civil rights activist**

Martin Luther King Jr.'s name was originally Michael King Jr., after his father, Michael King Sr. But, when the elder King took a trip to Germany, he was so impressed by Martin Luther (1483–1546) that he changed both his and his son's names in honor of the Protestant reformer. So Michael King Jr. became Martin Luther King Jr. (If you understood that the first time you read it, give yourself a pat on the back.)

Both his grandfather and his father were Baptist ministers, so it's no surprise that the younger King decided this was his vocation, too. He whizzed through school, skipping two grades, studied, and earned his PhD by the age of 25. He was soon the pastor of a Baptist church in Montgomery, Alabama. Meanwhile, he also became a member of the executive committee of the National Association for the Advancement of Colored People.

In 1955, segregation meant that in Alabama black people had to sit at the back of buses in seats labeled "for colored." If there weren't enough seats for white people, then black people had to stand so whites could sit down. On December 1 that year, when the bus driver asked a woman named Rosa Parks to give up her seat for a white man, she refused. In court, she was fined for breaking the law that allowed the bus driver to assign seats. She refused to pay. The fine was illegal, she said.

Step forward, Martin Luther King Jr.

He led a boycott of Montgomery's buses to force a change in the law. It was a peaceful protest, but even so, King was arrested and his home was bombed. Still, the protestors kept going, and at last—after 381 days—the U.S. Supreme Court ruled against Montgomery's segregation law. The civil rights protestors had won! But now they had to keep the ball rolling, and the Southern Christian Leadership Conference (SCLC) was formed to continue the fight for African-American civil rights. King was elected as the SCLC's president. He would be the man to lead them.

It wouldn't be a violent fight—that wasn't King's style. Like Gandhi (see page 40), he was a dedicated follower of nonviolence. Civil rights needed a healthy dose of public awareness, because the problem was that not enough people knew about the struggle for black equality. If they did, they too would help bring about change.

So King made speech after speech—thousands of them. He organized peaceful marches to highlight the injustices that black people faced daily. When police attacked protestors in Birmingham, Alabama, it was shown on the news, shocking people across the United States.

In 1963, one hundred years after President Lincoln's Emancipation Proclamation (see page 32), 250,000 black and white people marched on Washington, DC, to call for more black civil rights. At the Lincoln Memorial, King gave his famous "I Have a Dream" speech and inspired a nation.

The Civil Rights Act of 1964 banned discrimination against people based on their race, color, religion, or national origin. The same year, Martin Luther King Jr. was awarded the Nobel Peace Prize. Tragically, four years later, he was assassinated by white supremacist James Earl Ray.

STAND OUT, LIKE MARTIN LUTHER KING JR.!

Q It's just not fair. There are tons of students at school that speak English as a second language, yet none of them has been given a speaking part in the school play. The teachers say that they've simply chosen the best actors, but you don't believe them. How do you stand up, like Martin Luther King Jr.?

A He'd confront the teachers, of course. He'd explain that they may have chosen the most fluent speakers, but it doesn't mean they're the best actors. They might be missing out on a future movie star, just because their English isn't great (yet). And besides, how are those that speak English as a second language going to get any better if they don't have a chance to perform? Finally, he'd ask them to look at all the students again, because everyone deserves to be treated equally.

> Freedom is never voluntarily given by the oppressor; it must be demanded by the oppressed.

MARTIN LUTHER KING JR.

ANNE FRANK

EXTRAORDINARY DIARIST

Between 1942 and 1944, it was very, very dangerous for Anne Frank to stand up and speak out. She was one of eight Jews hiding from the Nazis in secret rooms at 263 Prinsengracht in Amsterdam. The softest footstep or the slightest noise could have alerted the enemy to their presence. But there was something she *could* do. She'd been given a red-and-white checked diary for her thirteenth birthday. She could *write*.

NAME: *Annelies Marie Frank*

BORN: June 12, 1929   DIED: February or March 1945

NATIONALITY: German

PROFESSION: Diarist and writer

Anne Frank was born just as things were becoming really difficult for Jewish people in Germany. The Nazis treated Jews harshly, and when they came to power in 1933, Anne's father, Otto, decided to leave. The Frank family moved to Amsterdam in the Netherlands. There, they would be safe.

But in 1939, war broke out. And in 1940, the Nazis invaded the Netherlands. When the Dutch surrendered, the Franks were back to square one. Things became tough for Jews here, too: they were forced to wear a yellow Star of David to show that they were Jewish; they couldn't ride streetcars; they had to do their shopping between 3 p.m. and 5 p.m.; they had to stay at home between 8 p.m. and 6 a.m.; they couldn't go to theaters or cinemas or play sports. Anne and her sister, Margot, had to go to a Jewish school. Meanwhile, Jewish people couldn't own businesses, so Otto Frank signed his company over to two non-Jewish friends (but secretly continued to run it).

Two years later, things became much worse—Margot was called up by the Nazis. This meant that Margot was probably going to be sent to a deadly concentration camp. The Frank family didn't hang around. At once, they put their emergency plan into action. They went into hiding with Otto's business partner and his family at 263 Prinsengracht, the company building.

Anne called their hiding place the Secret Annex. Hidden behind a moveable bookcase at the top of the building, it was made up of five rooms and was big enough for two families. Once they were inside, they couldn't leave. No one could know that they were there or they might be reported to the Nazi authorities. So they had to make sure not to open the curtains during the day, in case the neighbors saw them. They had to stay quiet in case anyone in the offices heard them. They couldn't have survived without a few non-Jewish friends, including Miep Gies, who brought them food, clothes, books, and news from Amsterdam. No one else knew they were there.

It wasn't the easiest place for a teenager to live. Anne was scared they might be discovered. She missed the outside world, and she missed her cat, Moortje. There were a lot of arguments. Anne's release valve was her diary. "The nicest part is being able to write down all my thoughts and feelings; otherwise I'd absolutely suffocate," she wrote. She dreamed of becoming a famous journalist or a writer. And when she heard that the Dutch government wanted Dutch people to keep diaries and documents to remember the occupation, she rewrote sections of her diary in the hope that one day it would be published.

But on August 4, 1944, the Nazis stormed the annex. Everyone inside was sent to concentration camps. By the following year, Anne was dead.

Otto was the only one of the eight residents of the Secret Annex to survive. Afterward, Miep Gies gave him Anne's notebooks that she'd kept safely hidden. And in 1947, just as Anne had wanted, her diary was published.

The Diary of a Young Girl by Anne Frank has been translated into over 70 languages and read by millions around the world. It is a powerful and important book that makes sure no one forgets what happened. Thank goodness for Anne Frank.

STAND UP, LIKE ANNE FRANK!

Q *You've written in a diary for years, but you're starting to wonder if there's any point. No one will EVER want to read about anything you have to say. Your life is way too dull. How do you stand out, like Anne Frank?*

A Writing was the only thing Anne Frank could do to escape the smothering claustrophobia of life in the Secret Annex. You don't have that problem, thankfully. But that doesn't mean that anything you have to say is pointless. Anne Frank was in a terrible situation, but she was also a teenager. In her diary, she wrote about her emotions and feelings and all kinds of everyday stuff, as well as the grim details of life in hiding. So cut yourself some slack and keep writing. You'll be glad you did.

> "I hope I will be able to confide everything to you, as I have never been able to confide in anyone, and I hope you will be a great source of comfort and support."

ANNE FRANK

CORY AQUINO

ICON OF DEMOCRACY

Cory Aquino never wanted to be
president. Her husband, Ninoy, was
the ambitious one. He campaigned to
beat President Marcos—a leader widely
thought to be corrupt—and become the
president of the Philippines himself. But
when Ninoy Aquino was assassinated and
the Philippines became a dictatorship,
Cory had a choice: should she quietly
mourn her husband, or should she find
a way to finish what he started?

Maria Corazon "Cory" Aquino

Cory came from a privileged background. Her parents were the wealthy owners of huge sugar plantations, and she had an excellent education in the Philippines and the United States. A year into law school, she met a young man with a promising future: Nimoy Aquino. They got married and had five children, and when his political career took off, Cory supported her husband however she could. But she avoided the limelight. He was the ambitious one, not her.

But Ninoy Aquino was about to get into a lot of trouble. Ferdinand Marcos was the president of the Philippines. He had used highly questionable tactics to get into power and was very unpopular. Ninoy Aquino criticized Marcos and campaigned against him. But Marcos simply abolished democratic rule and became a dictator. Now no one could beat him in an election, because there wouldn't *be* any elections.

Ninoy was arrested and imprisoned for eight years before moving to the United States. When he returned to the Philippines, he was assassinated by soldiers as soon as he landed in Manila.

Cory was grief-stricken. In the Philippines, there was outrage. Instead of mourning alone, Cory allowed her husband's coffin to take part in a procession before the funeral. When two million people paid their respects to her husband, she began to wonder if there was enough support to bring back democracy to the Philippines. Perhaps *she* could do what her husband had died trying to achieve.

Cory organized demonstrations. She encouraged everyone to protest against the dictatorship. In addition to the usual voters, she targeted businesses and students, the rich and the poor. And when, two years later, Marcos suddenly called an election, Cory Aquino was the obvious choice to run against him.

When it became clear that Aquino was likely to win, it's said that President Marcos cheated— BIG time. He delayed the election results for three weeks. Then he tried to claim victory himself. Aquino challenged Marcos, calling for Filipinos to take part in peaceful protests, strikes, and boycotts to put pressure on him. Two million people took part, and the protests became known as the People Power Revolution. After four days, Marcos gave in. He fled to Hawaii with his family.

Cory Aquino was the new president. And the Philippines was a democracy once more.

STAND OUT, LIKE CORY AQUINO!

Q *There's a crisis at the local animal shelter: too many pets are being abandoned and the place is bursting. If any new animals arrive, there's no choice but to put them down. You're so upset that you can't think straight. How do you stand up, like Cory Aquino?*

A Cory Aquino would try to put her sadness aside and concentrate on the matter at hand. OK, so you can't adopt any pets, but maybe others can. She'd make sure that the animal shelter got a ton of publicity. And she might also launch an awareness campaign so that possible pet owners think twice before buying an animal that, next week, they might not want.

> " I've reached a point in life where it's no longer necessary to try to impress. If they like me the way I am, that's good. If they don't, that's too bad. "

CORY AQUINO

YASUTERU YAMADA

SENIOR SUPERSTAR

When a devastating tsunami crashed into northeastern Japan, 72-year-old Yasuteru Yamada watched the catastrophic event on the news. Like the rest of the world, he was horrified when he realized that the 130 ft. (40 m) waves had damaged the Fukushima Daiichi Nuclear Power Plant. But anyone who tried to fix it could be exposed to harmful radiation.

NAME: *Yasuteru Yamada*

BORN: circa 1939
NATIONALITY: Japanese
PROFESSION: Retired engineer

On March 11, 2011, Japan's largest recorded earthquake shook the northeastern part of the country. It measured 9.1 on the Richter scale, which is pretty much as big as they get. But it wasn't the earthquake that was deadly—it was the tsunami that followed. Towering waves hit the coast of Honshu, killing thousands of people and destroying thousands more homes.

After the tsunami hit the Fukushima Daiichi Nuclear Power Plant, the nuclear reactors were shut down as a safety measure. Nuclear reactors give off heat that is used to generate electricity. Even after they are switched off, they continue to produce heat for a long, long time. The problem at Fukushima was that the tsunami also damaged the backup generators, and the lack of power meant that the cooling systems stopped working. So the reactors overheated and began to melt down, releasing radiation.

This was VERY bad news.

Thousands of people living nearby were evacuated. Meanwhile, the nuclear reactors needed to be cooled somehow. But how could this be done when there was a threat of radiation for anyone who went near?

This is where Yasuteru Yamada comes in. The retired engineer was disturbed that the people working hard to cool the reactors could be exposed to dangerous levels of radiation. Even small amounts of radiation could cause cancers such as leukemia years later, and this situation could be much, much worse. Then he had an idea. Instead of sending young people to Fukushima to repair the nuclear power plant, why shouldn't he volunteer to go instead?

Yamada's thinking was cool, calm, and very logical. If the cancers caused by radiation developed very slowly, then older engineers and specialists should do the work. He was 72 years old. If he became ill years later, he would already have lived a long life, while a younger worker's life could be tragically cut short. It made complete sense.

On his blog, Yamada asked if there were any other over-60s who'd like to join him. Four hundred people volunteered! Together they formed the Skilled Veterans Corps—a group that had a message for the Japanese government and the owners of the Fukushima Daiichi Nuclear Power Plant: they were ready to help.

> " Volunteering to take the place of younger workers at the power station is not brave, but logical. "
>
> YASUTERU YAMADA

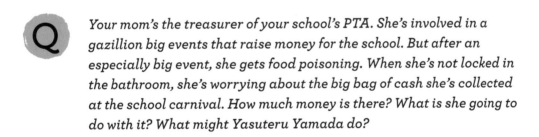

STAND UP, LIKE YASUTERU YAMADA!

Q *Your mom's the treasurer of your school's PTA. She's involved in a gazillion big events that raise money for the school. But after an especially big event, she gets food poisoning. When she's not locked in the bathroom, she's worrying about the big bag of cash she's collected at the school carnival. How much money is there? What is she going to do with it? What might Yasuteru Yamada do?*

A Yasuteru Yamada didn't think he was too old to help—and you're not too young. Yes, it's a lot of cash, but counting is easy-peasy. You can do that! Yamada would come up with a logical system for counting all the bills and coins and then get to work. He'd double-check and triple-check everything and then let someone else from the PTA know that the money is ready to be put in the bank. Then he might suggest that you take your mom a big drink of water and tell her that there's nothing to worry about.

STEPHEN HAWKING

SPACE-TIME WHIZ

Stephen Hawking was a math whiz. He was also a physics whiz. And a cosmology whiz. So, all in all, he was pretty smart. He spent years studying the universe and how it works, and knew an awful lot about space and time. So did the boy nicknamed Einstein in school just focus on being a brainiac? No. The great thing about Hawking is that as well as being super intelligent, he spoke and wrote about his discoveries in a way that *everyone* could understand.

Professor Stephen William Hawking

BORN: January 8, 1942   DIED: March 14, 2018

NATIONALITY: British

PROFESSION: Physicist, cosmologist, mathematician, and author

Stephen Hawking's parents wanted him to study medicine. Stephen wanted to study math. He won a scholarship to Oxford University, but studying math wasn't an option at his particular college, so he had to choose something else. And that was physics. He was so smart that he didn't need to put that much effort in to get top-level honors. (Do not try this at home. It only works if you're an actual genius.) Then he went on to the University of Cambridge, which was the place to be if you wanted to study cosmology. This is the part of astronomy that looks at how the universe works—from its very beginning to the distant future.

Meanwhile, Hawking discovered that he had an irreversible, life-changing illness. At 21, he was diagnosed with ALS—a type of motor neurone disease that affects the nerves that control movements like walking and talking, and even chewing. There was, and still is, no cure. Doctors didn't expect him to live long.

They were wrong.

Although Hawking's speech worsened and he had to start using a wheelchair when it became difficult for him to walk he was determined to carry on with his life and his cosmology studies.

Hawking thought a lot about huge subjects, including black holes, the big bang, the event horizon, matter, general relativity, quantum theory, space-time, and many, many other concepts that sound as if they belong in science fiction rather than science fact. He worked with other cosmologists to untangle old ideas and consider new ones. He even had a type of radiation named after him—Hawking radiation.

Meanwhile, Hawking was working his way up the academic ladder. He earned his doctorate. He got one great job after another. It was a huge honor when he was elected a fellow of the Royal Society, like other science whizzes Isaac Newton, Charles Darwin, and Albert Einstein. When a computer company invented a speech-generating device that meant Hawking could communicate by moving his cheek, he could give lectures, too! He also wrote really smart academic books about cosmology.

The thing was, most people didn't have a clue what any of these really smart academic books were talking about, because they were written for other really smart academics to read. So Hawking had a genius idea. He decided to write books about cosmology that nonscientists could understand.

In _A Brief History of Time_, Hawking explained all the very latest ideas about the universe that cosmologists were excited about. The book was aimed at readers who knew nothing about cosmology. It was an instant best-seller, translated into over 30 languages and selling over 10 million copies worldwide. That's a lot of readers who were pleased that he spoke out.

STAND OUT, LIKE STEPHEN HAWKING!

Q *Your homework makes no sense at all. Nada. Zero. Zilch. How on Earth can you answer the questions if you don't understand them? And how can you tell your teacher that you don't understand them? It'll look as if you weren't paying attention in class! What might Stephen Hawking say?*

A Stephen Hawking wrote books so that people could understand complicated concepts. There's no way on earth—or in space—that he'd want you to be scratching your head, especially if there was someone else who could make everything clear. So ask your classmates or a parent if they can help. And if they can't, then pluck up the courage to go back and ask the teacher to explain it again. They won't mind. Just like Hawking, they want you to know more.

"However difficult life may seem, there is always something you can do and succeed at.

STEPHEN HAWKING

MUHAMMAD ALI

THE GREATEST

Muhammad Ali was a legend inside the boxing ring and outside it. He achieved worldwide fame as a professional boxer. He had speed, stamina, and skill. He was smart too—and very, very funny. But when he stood up for his beliefs and refused to do his military service in the United States, he was banned from boxing for three years. His popularity plummeted. Could he bounce back? He could and he did, magnificently.

NAME: *Cassius Marcellus Clay Jr. / Muhammad Ali*

BORN: January 17, 1942   DIED: June 3, 2016

NATIONALITY: American

PROFESSION: Boxer and activist

When Cassius Clay grew up in Kentucky, people were segregated according to their skin color. He suffered discrimination simply because he was black. When he was 12, a police officer encouraged him to box. Clay was a natural. After a string of amateur fights, he won Olympic gold in the light heavyweight category in Rome in 1960.

Clay became a professional boxer, as famous for his personality as for his sparring skills. Acting like the world's biggest show-off, with a twinkle in his eye, he called himself "the Greatest." Some people couldn't stand this; others loved it. But it worked: everyone was interested in him. In 1960, he challenged Sonny Liston, the world heavyweight champion. He wasn't expected to win, but he did! Cassius Clay was the new world champion.

Two days later, he joined the Nation of Islam—a group of black Muslims. His new name was Muhammad Ali. He said that Cassius Clay was a slave name. He didn't choose it and he didn't want it. Now he was Muhammad Ali—a free name.

For three years, Ali ruled the boxing ring . . . until he was called up to join the U.S. Army. He didn't want to take part in the Vietnam War and became a conscientious objector—refusing to fight because it was against his beliefs. Many were appalled by his behavior. He was stripped of his heavyweight title and banned from boxing for three years. He was arrested and narrowly avoided jail. However, others were impressed by his stand. Before long, many more began to protest against a war that was becoming more and more unpopular.

Meanwhile, Ali highlighted the importance of black civil rights. Admired and supported by civil rights activists Malcolm X and Martin Luther King Jr., he made millions of African Americans feel proud of who they were and proud to fight for their rights. "I am America," he said. "I am the part you won't recognize. But get used to me—black, confident, cocky; my name, not yours; my religion, not yours; my goals, my own. Get used to me."

At last, he was allowed to box again. It took him three years, but he became heavyweight champion of the world once more. After losing the title to Leon Spinks, he won the rematch, winning the championship for a record-breaking third time.

After his retirement, Ali announced that he had Parkinson's disease, which affected his movement and speech. But he kept on making public appearances, supporting charities and good causes. He was named a United Nations Messenger of Peace. He was also awarded the Presidential Medal of Freedom. In 1996, he was chosen to light the Olympic flame in Atlanta.

STAND UP, LIKE MUHAMMAD ALI!

Q *Every weekend, Dad takes you and your brother out. This week it's the zoo. But you turn Dad down — you don't think animals should live in captivity. Your brother is furious. He desperately wanted to go, and now you've ruined everything. He'll never speak to you again. How do you stand up, like Muhammad Ali?*

A Ali proved that he didn't give a jot what others thought of him. He stuck up for his beliefs, even when they made him very, very unpopular. So he'd probably tell you to stick to your guns. Your dad will have other ideas up his sleeve. And don't worry about your brother. He'll come around. Besides, how's he going to irritate you if he's not speaking to you?

"FLOAT LIKE A BUTTERFLY; STING LIKE A BEE.

MUHAMMAD ALI

MARSHA P. JOHNSON

TRANSGENDER STAR

The first thing that stands out in photos of Marsha P. Johnson is her huge smile. She looks so utterly thrilled to be who she is and proud of what she's achieved. And rightly so. She was a transgender icon. She was an LGBTQ rights activist who took part in the Stonewall Riots. She helped young people who were homeless because their families couldn't deal with the fact that they were transgender. She spoke up for AIDS patients. She was truly a star as bright as her smile.

NAME: *Malcolm Michaels Jr. / Marsha P. Johnson*

BORN: **August 24, 1945**   DIED: **July 6, 1992**

NATIONALITY: **American**

PROFESSION: **Transgender icon and gay rights activist**

She was born Malcolm Michaels Jr. But ever since she was very young, Johnson liked to dress as a girl. It wasn't until she left home and moved to Greenwich Village in New York City that she was able to live by her own rules. She gave herself a brand-new name, too—Marsha P. Johnson. The "P" stood for "Pay it no mind," because that's what she replied when anyone asked her if she was a man or a woman or gay or straight. What she meant was—ignore it! Whatever she was, it really didn't matter.

In addition to waiting tables, she worked as a drag queen—an entertainer who performs in flamboyant women's clothes, wearing oodles of spectacular makeup. She was well known for wearing bright, colorful flowers in her hair and wild, wacky hats. She looked FABULOUS.

But life was anything but easy for Johnson and members of the LGBTQ (lesbian, gay, bisexual, transgender, and queer) community. They suffered from prejudice and discrimination. And many people acted as if there was something wrong with them. (Unfortunately, this is still often true today.) They weren't even allowed to marry someone of the same sex. (This is not true today!)

Then the Stonewall Riots happened.

The Stonewall Inn was a gay club at the very center of the LGBTQ world. Members of the community were not welcome in many places, but this was somewhere they could meet up without worrying about being harassed. It was somewhere they felt safe. So when the police raided the club on June 28, 1969, there was an uproar. When the police started arresting employees and beating up customers, Johnson was one of the first to fight back. Crowds soon gathered outside the club. They were outraged, and soon rioting broke out between the police and protestors. Six days of clashes and demonstrations followed. Because of her actions, Johnson became a symbol for the LGBTQ rights movement from then on.

Together, Johnson and her friend Sylvia Rivera founded STAR (Street Transvestite Action Revolutionaries), an organization that helped the homeless in the LGBTQ community by feeding them and giving them shelter whenever possible. Meanwhile, Johnson did whatever she could to help those living with AIDS. In 1980, she appeared at the very front of New York City's Gay Pride Parade.

In 1992, when she was just 46, Marsha P. Johnson died in mysterious circumstances. She drowned in the Hudson River: to this day no one knows for certain what happened. In 2016, Stonewall Inn became the first LGBTQ national monument in the United States, dedicated to the LGBTQ civil rights movement. President Barack Obama declared that it was a place for the LGBTQ community "to assemble for marches and parades, expressions of grief and anger, and celebrations of victory and joy."

How many years has it taken people to realize that we are all brothers and sisters and human beings in the human race? I mean how many years does it take people to see that? We're all in this rat race together!

MARSHA P. JOHNSON

STAND OUT, LIKE MARSHA P JOHNSON!

One of your friends has told you that they think they might be gay. You're not sure what to do or what to say. How do you stand up, like Marsha P. Johnson?

Come on. Get with the program. She would tell you to keep on treating them exactly the same as before. Whether they're gay or not doesn't make the TINIEST bit of difference. They're still your friend, and that's what's important. What they *are* going to need is your support. Be there if they need you. And be prepared to help them if things get tough. That's what Marsha P. Johnson was excellent at doing. You can be, too.

KATHRINE SWITZER

MARATHON WOMAN

Not so long ago, the Boston Marathon used to be a men-only event. Women weren't allowed to enter, even if they wanted to. They were thought to be too frail and too fragile. They were simply not up to it. Bobbi Gibb proved them wrong when she ran the marathon illegally in 1966. Meanwhile, Kathrine Switzer thought women needed to go one step further. They should be able to take part in the Boston Marathon legally, just like men.

NAME: *Kathrine Virginia "Kathy" Switzer*
BORN: January 5, 1947   NATIONALITY: American
PROFESSION: Runner and author

In school, Kathrine Switzer wanted to be a cheerleader. But her father said that wasn't right: cheerleaders cheered for other people, and other people should be cheering for *her*. So Switzer became a runner instead. At her college there was no women's cross-country team, so she trained with the men, which is how she met Arnie Briggs. He was the coach, and he'd already run the Boston Marathon. Inspired by him, Switzer decided that she wanted to run it, too.

But women weren't allowed to take part in the marathon, and Switzer's own coach didn't believe she could do it. She was facing an uphill struggle if she wanted to participate. A woman named Bobbi Gibb had completed it illegally the year before, leaping out of a bush near the starting line. But Gibb's achievement wasn't recognized. Switzer wanted her own run to count.

The Boston Marathon is the world's oldest marathon. It first took place in 1897. Competitors have to prove they are fast enough before they're allowed to register. And even then the race is limited to 30,000 runners. Basically, running the Boston Marathon is a fairly big deal.

Switzer's coach told her that if she could prove to him she could run the distance, he'd take her to Boston. Fired with enthusiasm, she did just that. So that left only the fact that women couldn't take part. On her registration, Switzer used her initials instead of her first name. This was how she signed her name. But it also meant that no one knew that she was a woman.

Wearing the number 261, Switzer set off. But she'd barely run 2 mi. (3 km) when a furious race official grabbed her and tried to pull her off the course. Switzer was terrified. But she got away and kept going—completing the marathon with a time of 4 hours 20 minutes. She'd done it!

After the race, Switzer became completely focused on women's right to run. She campaigned so that women could officially enter the Boston Marathon. She became director of the Women's Sports Foundation. She won the New York City Marathon. Thanks in part to her efforts, the 1984 Olympic Games included a women's marathon, helping change public opinion of women runners. She also wrote a book and began 261 Fearless—a global movement that aims to empower women through running. And Switzer hasn't stopped running since. Fifty years after she first ran the Boston Marathon, she ran it again, at age 70.

STAND UP, LIKE KATHRINE SWITZER!

Q *It's unfair. Your dad has this outdated idea that girls should be ladylike and terribly refined. So while it's all right for your brother to roll around on a football field, it's somehow not OK for you to play the sport, too. How might you stand up, like Kathrine Switzer?*

A Switzer might just play regardless, to show your dad how it's done. Or maybe she'd be more subtle. She might suggest you show your dad all the athletic women who've excelled in sports traditionally dominated by men. The same applies if you're a boy who wants to take part in an activity that's seen as being "girly," of course. Either way, stand up like Kathrine did! Send stereotypes back where they belong . . . to history!

JULIANE KOEPCKE

SURVIVOR

Christmas Eve 1971 was not a good day for 17-year-old Juliane Koepcke. After taking off from Lima, the capital of Peru, her plane flew into a thunderstorm. A lightning bolt hit a fuel tank, which exploded, ripping off one wing. The plane crashed . . . but Koepcke didn't crash with it. Somehow, she was separated from the aircraft and, still strapped into her seat, she plummeted from the sky. Unbelievably, she survived! That was the good news. The bad news was that she now had to find her way out of the Amazon rain forest—on her own.

Juliane Koepcke's parents were both top-level zoologists who worked at a natural history museum in Lima, Peru. When they decided to set up a research station in Panguana in the Amazon rain forest, Juliane went, too. For 18 months, she was homeschooled. Juliane had a second classroom: the rain forest. There, she learned about the huge array of amazing wildlife that surrounded her—insects, animals, birds, and so, so many plants. She also learned survival skills. But the education authorities didn't approve of Juliane's homeschooling and so she had to return to school in Lima. She graduated when she was 17.

On Christmas Eve, Juliane and her mother were flying back to the research station after Juliane's graduation ball when disaster struck and the plane crashed.

When Juliane woke on Christmas Day, she was astonished to be alive. Miraculously, her only injuries were a broken collarbone, a swollen eye, and cuts on her legs. It's thought that the aircraft seat protected her, while the dense canopy of the rain forest slowed her fall. She was completely alone in the rain forest. And she needed to get out of there.

Koepcke knew the rain forest, so she didn't feel scared. Plus, she knew how to take care of herself. But putting survival skills into practice, especially when you've just been dumped out of the sky and all you have to eat is a bag of candy, is not easy. The first thing she did was to find a stream so that she'd have water to drink. Then, if she followed the water, it would lead to a river and hopefully civilization—as long as she could avoid the caimans, piranhas, snakes, and poisonous frogs on the way.

Koepcke followed the stream through the rain forest, clambering over tree trunks and forcing her way through thick undergrowth. She was wearing a thin dress and only one shoe, and she'd lost her glasses in the crash, so it was difficult to see where she was going. She knew that many plants in the jungle were poisonous, so she didn't dare eat any of them.

After a few days—she was starting to lose count—Koepcke heard the sound of a hoatzin. This was wonderful! She knew that these birds were found near large areas of water, where she might find people! She followed the sound and did find a wide river . . . but there was no one there.

Doggedly, she went on. It was difficult to walk along the riverbank because it was so crowded with plants, so she swam instead. By now, she was sunburned, weak, and very, very hungry.

Then she saw a boat, and shelter, too. But still there were no people. So she slept. The following evening, after 11 days in the rain forest, she was found by three forestry workers. She'd done it! She hadn't given up. She'd *survived*.

Juliane Koepcke still visits the research station in Panguana, where she once lived. It's now a conservation area.

STAND OUT, LIKE JULIANE KOEPCKE!

Q *You want to join the Scouts, but your friends say it's a waste of time. What's the point of camping and hiking and caving and rappelling? Why do you need to learn how to tie a gazillion knots? Why can't you play video games like a normal person? How might Juliane Koepcke stand out?*

A After surviving everything that the Amazon rain forest threw at her, it's highly likely that Juliane would tell you to go for it. Scouting is about way more than tying knots. Just ask any of the millions of Scouts around the world.

> " I'm trying to save the rain forest that saved my life. "

JULIANE KOEPCKE

J. K. ROWLING

OUTSPOKEN AUTHOR

Unless you've been living in a closet under the stairs since 1997, you'll already know that J. K. Rowling is one of the most famous authors of all time. Her seven Harry Potter books have sold more than half a billion copies and been translated into 80 different languages. They've all been made into box-office-smashing movies. There's a spin-off play, too. And she writes for adults. So surely the millions of words she's written mean there's been no time for anything else . . .? Not at all.

NAME: *Joanne Rowling*

BORN: July 31, 1965

NATIONALITY: British PROFESSION: Author

After leaving school, Joanne Rowling did a degree, lived in Paris, worked for human rights organization Amnesty International, taught English in Portugal, got married, had a daughter, got divorced, and moved to Edinburgh, Scotland. But meanwhile, she also had something magical on her mind: Harry Potter®. After the idea popped into her head on a delayed train, she spent years planning the entire series of books. By the time she reached Edinburgh—a single mother with no money and no job—she'd written the first three chapters of the first Harry Potter® book. She wrote the rest of the book in cafés around Edinburgh.

At last, the manuscript was finished and Rowling sent it to a literary agent. They sent it back. So she sent it to another. The agent liked it—hurray!—and sent it to a publisher. The publisher sent it back. The agent sent it to another publisher. Back it came again. Twelve different publishers said no to the first Harry Potter® book. But the next publisher was Bloomsbury and they said **YES**, and the book was an instant bestseller. (If you've ever wondered where the K in J. K. Rowling comes from, it stands for Kathleen—Rowling's grandmother's name. The publisher worried that boys wouldn't want to read a book by a woman, so they hid her identity behind initials.)

From then on, every time a new Harry Potter® book was published, the fans went wild. Every time a new Harry Potter® movie was released, they went wild again. There's now a studio tour and a theme park. There's even a Platform 9 ¾ at King's Cross railway station in London, England. (And if you don't know why this is important, you really must've been living in a closet under the stairs.)

Rowling doesn't just write children's fiction. Her first adult novel was *A Casual Vacancy*. Then she went on to write the Cormoran Strike detective fiction series, which was published under the name of Robert Galbraith, but she was soon revealed to be the real author. All of the books have now been adapted for TV.

With such huge success, you'd expect Rowling to be a gazillionaire. Except she isn't, because she gives so much to charity. She says that she hasn't forgotten what it feels like to worry about paying bills. And as one of the most famous people in the world, she uses her celebrity to shine a spotlight on good causes. She is the president of Gingerbread—a British nonprofit organization working with single-parent families, providing advice and practical support. She founded Lumos— named after the light-giving spell in the Harry Potter® series—an international nonprofit that aims to help the millions of children in orphanages around the world find new homes. She supports so many nonprofits that in 2017 she was made a Companion of Honour by the Duke of Cambridge for her services to literature and philanthropy—the wish to promote the welfare of others.

STAND UP, LIKE J. K. ROWLING!

Q *You're being bullied. You don't want to tell anyone, because you're worried that the bullies will find out and the bullying will get even worse. How might J. K. Rowling stand up?*

A It's a well known fact that J. K. Rowling loathes bullying. She was bullied at school, so she knows how awful it can be. Nowadays she blasts them with a witty comeback, which makes the rest of the world laugh and the bullies feel stupid. So prepare a few witty remarks to throw back at the bully the next time they say something. And they'll probably be the only one who won't find it funny! (But why not tell a teacher while you're at it? They're pretty good at dealing with bullies too.)

> We do not need magic to change the world. We carry all the power we need inside ourselves already: we have the power to imagine better.

J.K. ROWLING

WHICH PROTESTOR ARE YOU?

Answer these multiple-choice questions to find out which fabulous person you are most like. Make a note of how many As, Bs, Cs, Ds, or Es you score and then (and NOT before) turn to page 110 to reveal your protest twin.

1 Your school has decided to run its own online newspaper and it needs volunteers. You're excited. But which job is for you?

a) You're going to write the healthy living section. It's the only part of a newspaper worth reading.

b) You'd like to be in charge, but if someone else is desperate to do the job, you're not going to have an argument about it.

c) OK, so you'd like to be a journalist and an editor and an illustrator, and perhaps you could help with the publicity, too.

d) You're going to write the headlines to highlight local issues.

e) You're in charge. End of conversation.

2 For your English homework you have to write about someone who's inspired you. Who do you choose?

a) Your mom—she's done so much to be proud of.

b) There are so many good people to choose from . . . How do you decide?!

c) Your favorite teacher of all time.

d) Anyone who stands up for what they believe in.

e) Well, whoever it is, it's not going to be a Roman.

3 When you're not protesting, how do you relax?

a) Traveling the world!

b) You meditate.

c) You sing or dance or write or act or read a really good book.

d) You box.

e) Relaxing is for wimps. You fight.

4 The local animal shelter desperately needs funds. How do you help?

a) Crowdfunding is the way to go. You set up a page for people to start giving immediately.

b) Not enough people know the animal shelter is in trouble, and you're going to change that by holding a peaceful demonstration outside the center.

c) You write a play that you and your classmates perform to raise funds.

d) It's time for action! Now! And you're taking it to the top. You encourage all of your friends to join you in a demonstration outside city hall.

e) You make appointments with all of the local businesses and tell them bluntly that they need to do something. NOW.

5 If you were an animal, which one would you be?

a) An orangutan. Or any other amazingly caring mother in the animal kingdom.

b) A swan. You look calm, but there's a lot going on underneath.

c) A chameleon. You're different every day.

d) A lion. You're regal and strong.

e) A tiger. You're FIERCE.

6 You want to stay out late. Your mom says, "NO." What do you do?

a) Oh well. Staying in isn't that much of a problem. You'll go out another night.

b) Stage a sit-in in front of the television. You're not going to disobey your mom, but BOY is she going to know that you're unhappy about it.

c) You're good with words. You choose all the most persuasive ones you know to try to get your mom to change her mind.

d) You come up with a list of reasons why it's a good thing for you to go out, and then present them to your mom.

e) You haven't listened to anyone in a position of authority yet, and you're not going to start now.

7 What's your favorite after-school club?

a) First aid.

b) Yoga.

c) Drama. Or dance. Or filmmaking. Or acting. Or public speaking. Or poetry. Or book club. Or singing. Or any one of a billion other arty things you haven't tried yet.

d) Anything to do with politics.

e) Kickboxing.

8 How long would you be prepared to support something that you believe in?

a) As long as anyone needs help, you'll be there.

b) As long as it takes.

c) Your whole life.

d) Until you achieve what you set out to do.

e) Let's face it. You're pretty hardcore. It's not going to take that long to get what you want.

Mostly a.

You're caring and trustworthy, just like Mary Seacole.
(See page 28.)

Mostly b.

Like you, Mahatma Gandhi didn't have to be violent to get things done.
(See page 40.)

Mostly c.

Maya Angelou did it all. Be like Maya!
(See page 64.)

Mostly d.

Nelson Mandela was strong, determined, and very patient. Will you change the world, too?
(See page 56.)

Mostly e.

Psst. The ancient Romans are gone now. It's OK to be a little calmer than Boudicca.
(See page 12.)

TIMELINE

1759–1797
Mary Wollstonecraft

1805–1881
Mary Seacole

1809–1865
Abraham Lincoln

1910–2008
Irena Sendler

1918–2013
Nelson Mandela

1921–1943
Sophie Scholl

circa 1939
Yasuteru Yamada

1942–2018
Stephen Hawking

1942–2016
Muhammad Ali

**circa 109 BC–
71 BC**
Spartacus

**circa AD 30–
AD 60/61**
Boudicca

1533–1603
Elizabeth I

1564–1642
Galileo Galilei

1865–1915
Edith Cavell

1869–1948
Mahatma
Gandhi

1880–1968
Helen Keller

1903–1950
George Orwell

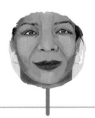

1928–2014
Maya Angelou

1929–1968
Martin Luther
King Jr.

1929–1945
Anne Frank

1933–2009
Cory Aquino

1945–1992
Marsha P.
Johnson

1947
Kathrine
Switzer

1954
Juliane
Koepcke

1965
J. K. Rowling

INDEX